PLANET
HULK
WORLDBREAKER

PLANET HULK

WORLDBREAKER

GREG PAK
WRITER

MANUEL GARCIA
PENCILER

CAM SMITH
INKER

CHRIS SOTOMAYOR
COLOR ARTIST

VC's JOE CARAMAGNA
LETTERER

CARLO PAGULAYAN, JASON PAZ & CHRIS SOTOMAYOR
COVER ART

"SKAAR, SON OF HULK"
WRITER **GREG PAK** | ARTIST **RAMÓN F. BACHS**
COLOR ARTIST **CHRIS SOTOMAYOR** | LETTERER **VC's JOE CARAMAGNA**

ASSISTANT EDITOR **MIKEY J. BASSO** | ASSOCIATE EDITOR **DANNY KHAZEM**
EDITOR **MARK PANICCIA**

HULK CREATED BY **STAN LEE & JACK KIRBY**

COLLECTION EDITOR: **DANIEL KIRCHHOFFER**
ASSISTANT MANAGING EDITOR: **MAIA LOY**
ASSOCIATE MANAGER, TALENT RELATIONS: **LISA MONTALBANO**
DIRECTOR, PRODUCTION & SPECIAL PROJECTS: **JENNIFER GRÜNWALD**
VP PRODUCTION & SPECIAL PROJECTS: **JEFF YOUNGQUIST**
BOOK DESIGNER: **RODOLFO MURAGUCHI**
SVP PRINT, SALES & MARKETING: **DAVID GABRIEL**
EDITOR IN CHIEF: **C.B. CEBULSKI**

PLANET HULK: WORLDBREAKER. Contains material originally published in magazine form as PLANET HULK: WORLDBREAKER (2022) #1-5. First printing 2023. ISBN 978-1-302-93473-6. Published by MARVEL WORLDWIDE, INC., a subsidiary of MARVEL ENTERTAINMENT, LLC. OFFICE OF PUBLICATION: 1290 Avenue of the Americas, New York, NY 10104. **Printed in Canada.** KEVIN FEIGE, Chief Creative Officer; DAN BUCKLEY, President, Marvel Entertainment; DAVID BOGART, Associate Publisher & SVP of Talent Affairs; TOM BREVOORT, VP, Executive Editor; NICK LOWE, Executive Editor, VP of Content, Digital Publishing; DAVID GABRIEL, VP of Print & Digital Publishing; SVEN LARSEN, VP of Licensed Publishing; MARK ANNUNZIATO, VP of Planning & Forecasting; JEFF YOUNGQUIST, VP of Production & Special Projects; ALEX MORALES, Director of Publishing Operations; DAN EDINGTON, Director of Editorial Operations; RICKEY PURDIN, Director of Talent Relations; JENNIFER GRÜNWALD, Director of Production & Special Projects; SUSAN CRESPI, Production Manager; STAN LEE, Chairman Emeritus. For information regarding advertising in Marvel Comics or on Marvel.com, please contact Vit DeBellis, Custom Solutions & Integrated Advertising Manager, at vdebellis@marvel.com. For Marvel subscription inquiries, please call 888-511-5480. **Manufactured between 4/7/2023 and 5/9/2023 by SOLISCO PRINTERS, SCOTT, QC, CANADA.**

10987654321

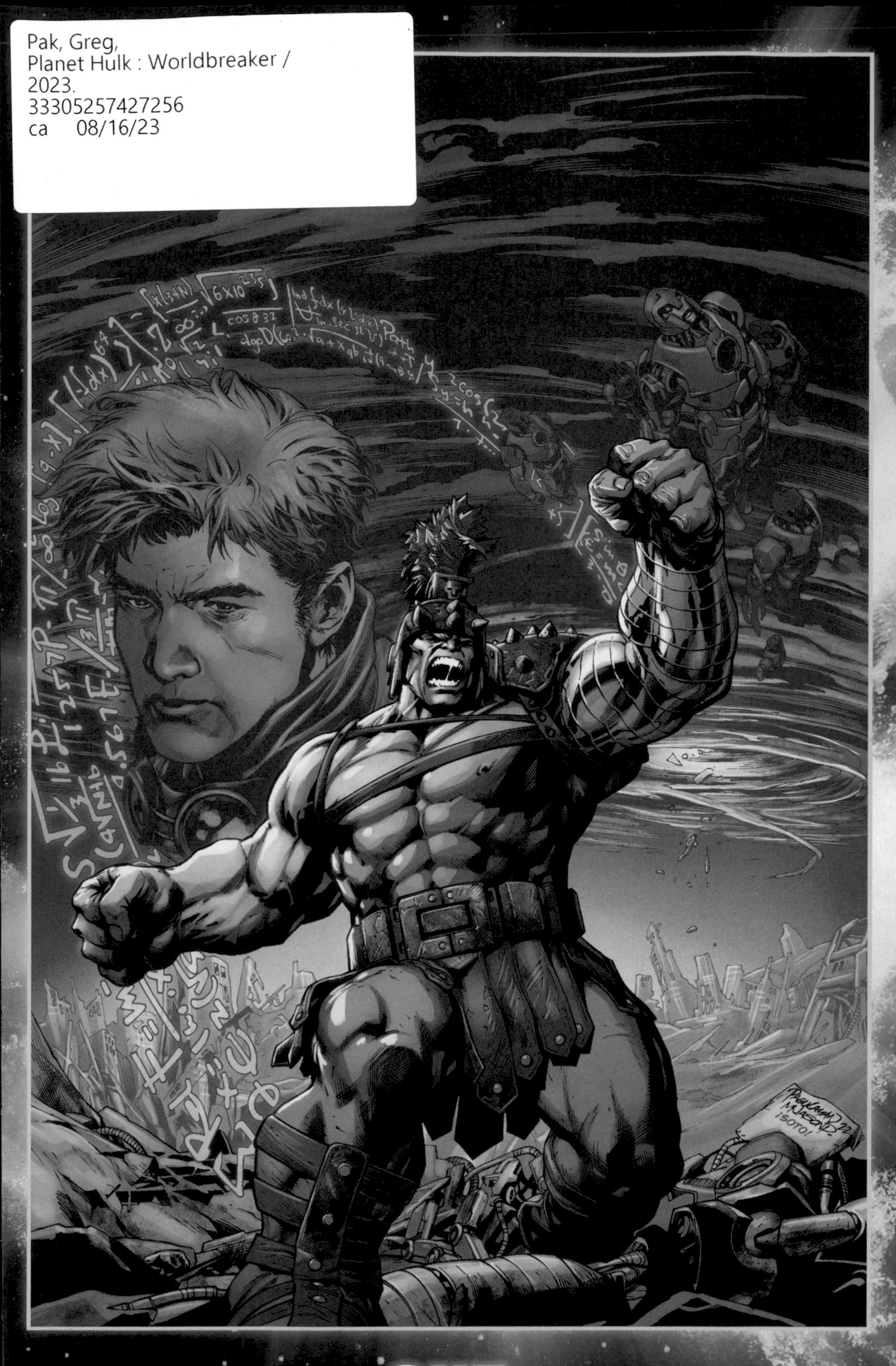

ONE

THIS IS THE STORY OF THE GREEN SCAR.
THE EYE OF ANGER.
THE WORLDBREAKER.
HAARG.
HOLKU.
HULK.
YOU KNOW THE OLD STORIES.
BUT AFTER ALL THESE GENERATIONS, THE QUESTION REMAINS THE SAME--
--WAS HE A HERO OR A MONSTER?
FINALLY, MY PEOPLE, I COME TO YOU WITH THE ANSWER...

PLANET SAKAAR. ONE THOUSAND YEARS FROM NOW.
...HE WAS A MONSTER.
AND SO WERE ALL THE HAARG WHO FOLLOWED HIM.
HAIL, GRAND PRIESTESS VENKIERA!
HAIL, GRAND PRIESTESS VENKIERA.
SOME OF YOU SOUND...
...LESS THAN CONVINCED.
THAT'S ALL RIGHT.
IT'S HARD TO ADMIT THE TRUTH, EVEN WHEN IT'S BEEN KICKING US IN THE FACE FOR CENTURIES.
THE HAARG SAID THEY GAVE US FREEDOM.
BUT LOOK AROUND YOU.
WHAT DID THEY REALLY GIVE US?
HERE IT COMES...

SHATTERED EARTH!
MOLTEN RIVERS!
ASHEN SKIES!
BEASTS DRIVEN MAD AND MURDEROUS BY UNNATURAL CHANGE...
...ALIEN VINES STRANGLING THE GOLDEN FIELDS OF OUR ANCESTORS...
...AND GREEN-SKINNED MONSTERS ROAMING AMONG US!
LET'S GO.

I'M SORRY, BALO. I THOUGHT WE COULD STAY THERE, MAYBE SLEEP IN AN ACTUAL BED FOR A FEW DAYS.
THAT'S OKAY, TALA.
IT'S NOT SAFE.
NO. BUT DON'T WORRY.
I'M ALWAYS GONNA WATCH OUT FOR--
OOH!
LOOK.
THAT'S A NICE ONE!
HM.
YOU...CAN HAVE THIS ONE.
OH, THANK YOU SO MUCH.
YOU'RE WELCOME.

HEY, THESE LOOK GOOD!
SNUFF SNURF
DON'T WORRY, IT'S ALL RIGHT.
MUNCH MUNCH
I KNOW...
"...YOU'RE ALWAYS GONNA KEEP ME SAFE."
IS THAT WHERE WE'RE GOING?
THE SKY CITY?
MAYBE.
IF THAT PRIESTESS HASN'T ALREADY GOTTEN--
THERE!

HAARG!
RUN!
YOU COME ANY CLOSER AND--
SKRRAAAK
AAAH!
KKRRRAAAKT
GAAAAAAH!

HUH. STILL STANDING?
YOU CHARGE THAT THING UP?
YES, I CHARGED IT UP. WHAT DO YOU THINK--?
YOU-- YOU CAN'T HURT ME.
BUT I CAN HURT YOU.
I'LL GIVE YOU ONE CHANCE TO RIDE AWAY.
OR YOU'LL SEE WHAT A HAARG CAN DO.
YAAA!
WHA--?
HA HA HA!
APPARENTLY, WHAT A HAARG CAN DO...
...IS NOT TOO MUCH.
KTHOKK
UKK!
EEEEEE
TCH. THIS ONE'S TOO OLD, CAPTAIN!
ALL RIGHT, THEN. KILL HER.

NO!
PTING
THAT FLUSHED HIM OUT!
GET HIM!
NO!
BALO!
RUN!
BLAAAMMM

WHADDAYA THINK, MADDY?
IS *THIS* THE ONE?
NAH...
...BUT WHAT ABOUT *THIS?*
NO, NO, NO, NOPE.
WAAAIT A MINUTE...
THIS MIGHT BE IT.
FIX IT, FIX IT, *FIX* IT...
...PUT IT ALL *TOGETHER*...
HAARG...
WHA--?

...HOLKU...
...EYE OF ANGER...
...SAKAARSON...
THAT'S-- THAT'S NOT ME!
...G-- G--
--GRANDPA...
...CHO...
GRANDPA?

HEY.
HI.
YOU GOT HIT POINT-BLANK BY AN OVERCRANKED SHI'AR NEURAL STINGER.
YOU SHOULD BE DEAD.
BUT YOU'RE STRONG.
NOT STRONG ENOUGH.
NOT LIKE YOU.
WHO...
...WHO DO YOU THINK I AM?
MY MOTHER TOLD ME WHERE YOU LIVED...
...BUT SHE SAID YOU'D BEEN THROUGH TOO MUCH.
SO I SHOULDN'T BOTHER YOU...
...UNLESS I DIDN'T HAVE ANY OTHER OPTION.
YOUR MOTHER...
GLORY.
SHE DIED LAST YEAR.
I THOUGHT...
...I THOUGHT SHE HAD MORE TIME.

SHE TOLD US NOT TO CRY.
SHE SAID SHE LIVED LONGER THAN ANYONE ELSE SHE KNEW.
EXCEPT YOU.
SHE SAID YOU SAVED THE WORLD.
NINE TIMES.
NO. JUST TWICE. ON MY OWN, ANYWAY.
THREE WERE MORE OF A...GROUP EFFORT.
THE REST WERE BANNER.
BANNER?
THE GREEN SCAR.
THE EYE OF ANGER.
THE WORLDBREAKER.
BUT THAT'S... YOU.
AND YOU'RE THE SAKAARSON, THE ONE WHO SAVED US ALL, NOT THE WORLDBR--
YOU HAVE NO IDEA.
UNINTENDED CONSEQUENCES.
WE BROKE TOO MANY THINGS.
BUT SHE SAID YOU--
WHAT IF A WILDEBOT'S ATTACKING A VILLAGE.
YOU SMASH IT. SAVE A THOUSAND PEOPLE...

...BUT THE BOT WAS POWERED BY AN ALIEN ENERGY SOURCE.
WHICH YOU RELEASED WHEN YOU SMASHED IT...
...AND FIFTY YEARS LATER, A HUNDRED PEOPLE IN THE VILLAGE HAVE DIED OF CANCER?
THAT'S...
...THAT'S NOT YOUR FAULT.
REALLY?
WHAT IF YOU LIVE A THOUSAND YEARS?
AND IT HAPPENS AGAIN AND AGAIN, IN TINY AND HUGE WAYS?
WHAT IF YOU COULD SEE THE RAMIFICATIONS OF EVERY MISTAKE YOU EVER MADE, AMPLIFIED OVER TIME, REVERBERATING THROUGH THE LIVES AND DEATHS OF HUNDREDS, OF THOUSANDS OF PEOPLE?
AND I'M JUST AMADEUS.
WHO WAS MOSTLY IN CONTROL.
IMAGINE...
...IMAGINE HOW BANNER FEELS.
SO NOW YOU JUST... FIX TOYS?
IT'S SAFER.
FOR EVERYONE.
THE PRIESTESS STOLE MY BROTHER.
HE'S ONLY FIVE.
IT'S NOT SAFER FOR HIM.

NO, GRANDPA, IT'S THIS WAY.
YOUR...
...YOUR BROTHER'S GREEN, RIGHT?
YYYESS?
OKAY, WAIT A MINUTE...
GRANDPA...
NO TIME. I KNOW.
YOU'RE SO WORRIED...
...BUT YOU'RE HUMORING ME.
THAT'S KIND OF YOU.
IT'S... IT'S ALL RIGHT. JUST...
...HURRY.
CLICK
HE'S THAT WAY.
AAAAND...
...HE'S ALIVE AND UNINJURED.
THEY'RE NOT ALL TOYS.

THERE IT IS. A SHADOW STARSHIP.
SMART OF THEM. THAT STONE'S VIRTUALLY IMPERVIOUS, EVEN AFTER ALL THESE--
HE'S IN THERE? AND HE'S ALL RIGHT?
AS FAR AS I CAN TELL.
LET'S GO, THEN.
HANG ON.
"HAARG SMASH," I KNOW.
BUT IF YOU HAVEN'T FIGURED IT OUT BY NOW...
...I WAS ALWAYS BEST KNOWN FOR USING MY BRAINS.
?
EEE?
HAW HAW HAW!
EEE?
EEE?
OH!

EEE!
HI.
THAT'S HIM!
ALL IN ONE PIECE, JUST LIKE I SAID.
HOW DO WE GET HIM OUT?
JUST A MINUTE-- LET'S SEE WHAT...
WHIIIINE
SOB
HELLO?
HELP!
GRANDPA! ALL THOSE KIDS!
WHAT ARE THEY DOING WITH THEM?
I DON'T KNOW.
BUT YOU GO TAKE COVER NOW...
...BECAUSE IT'S TIME FOR GRANDPA TO--

HAARG! DESTROY!
SKRRRAAAAAKKTT
GAAAAH!
HAARG! DESTROY!
G-GAMMA INHIBITORS!
THEY-- THEY PREPARED FOR US!
RUN!
SKRRRAAAAKKTT
SKRRAAAAKKTT
NO!
KID!
DON'T JUST SIT THERE, GRANDPA...
...SMASH!
RRRRRR...

GRRRRRAAAAAA!
SKRAAAAAKOOOOOOOOM
RRRAAAAAGGH!
FRRAAAKOOOOOOM
SKRRRRRRRAAAAAKK
AAAAAGH!

HAARG! DESTROY!
HAARG! DESTROY!
HAARG! DESTROY!
WE-- WE'RE NOT STRONG ENOUGH FOR THIS.
GOD HELP US...
...BUT WE NEED BANNER.
THE SAKAARSON.
NO...

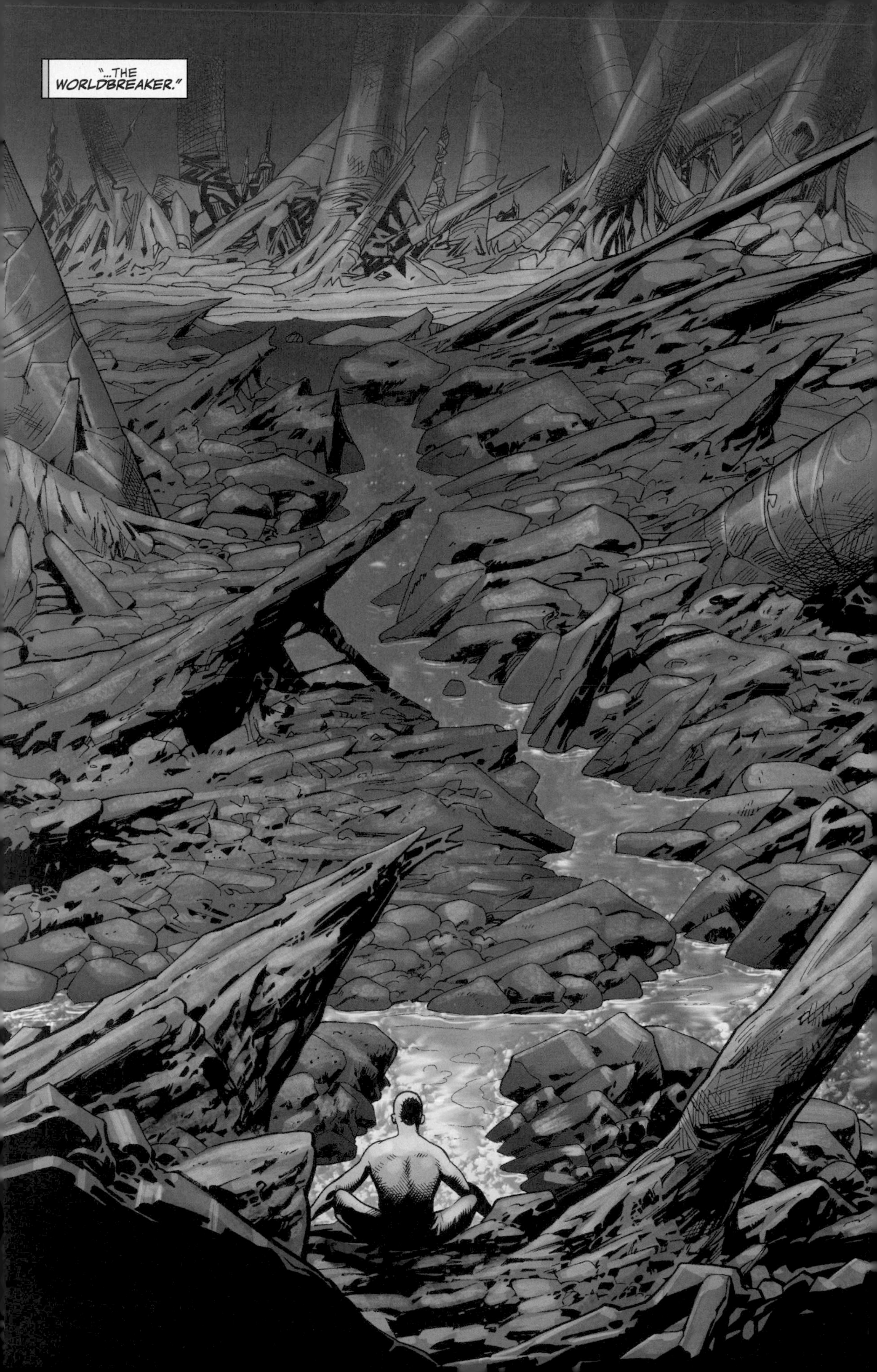
"...THE WORLDBREAKER."

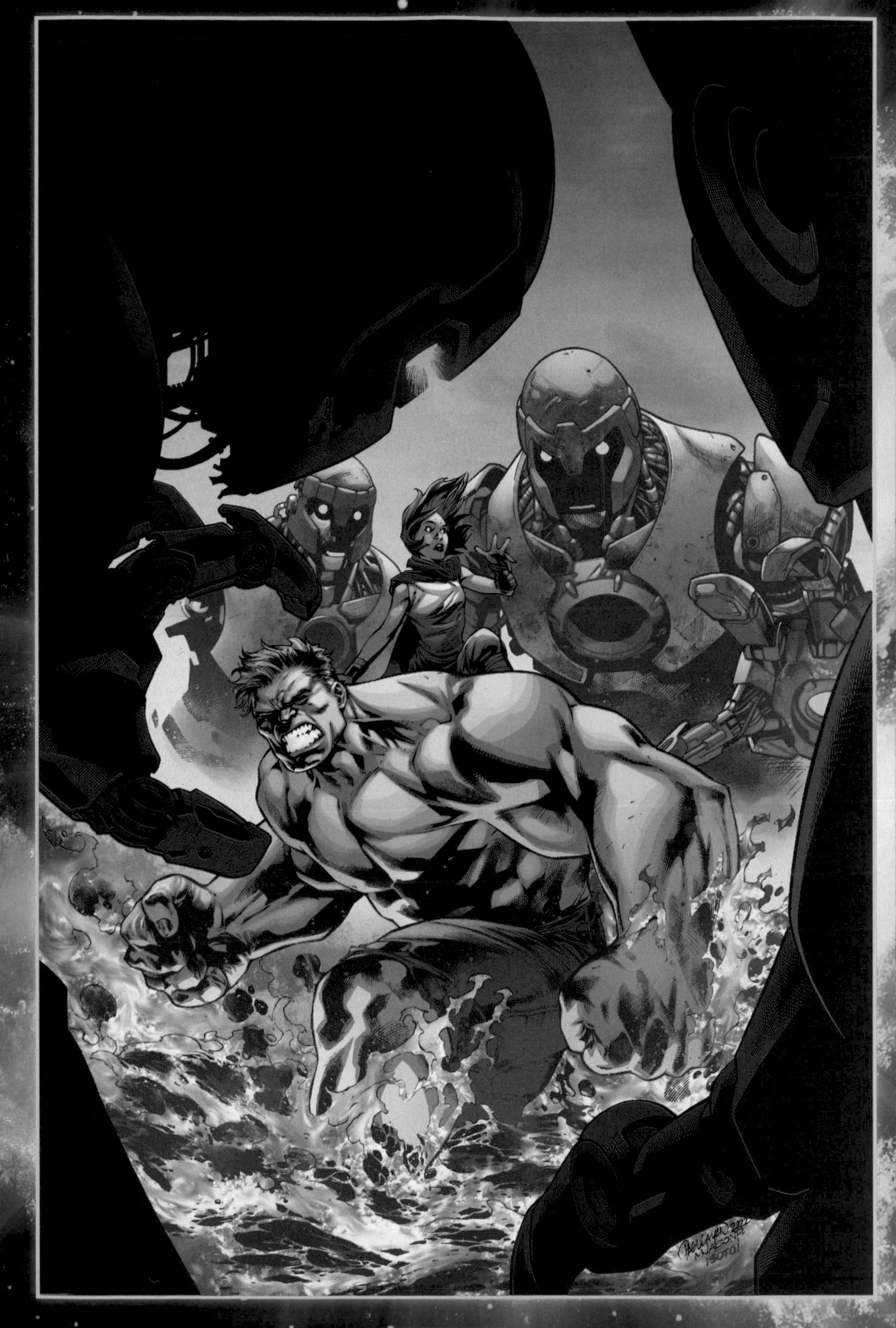

TWO

DESTROY!
ALL!
HAARG!
DESTROY!
ALL!
HAARG!
BRRZZZAAAM
GAAAAAH!
PLANET SAKAAR. A THOUSAND YEARS FROM NOW.
WH-WHAT ARE YOU DOING?
THEY'RE FIRING GAMMA INHIBITORS-- YOU'VE GOTTA STAY BEHIND ME!
NO, GRANDPA CHO--
BRRZZZAAAAM
--YOU GET BEHIND ME!

YOU--YOU CAN'T--
SKRRRRAAAKK
NNGH!
I CAN'T SMASH...
...BUT I'M STRONG IN MY OWN WAY.
YOU SURE ARE.
BUT YOU CAN'T BEAR THIS FOR LONG.
JUST A MINUTE...
COME ON, BRAIN.
COME ON.
I KNOW YOU GOT A LITTLE SOMETHING LEFT...
GGRRRAAAAAA!

DANGER! DANGER!
KTHOOOOOM
SKRRRAAAAKKT
DESTROY! ALL! HAARG!
HYAA!
WELL, THAT BARELY WORKED!
BUT IT WORKED!
BRRZZZAAM BRRRZZZAM

THE HAARG ARE ESCAPING, GRAND PRIESTESS!
YES, AFTER BREAKING THE WORLD AGAIN.
BUT THEY'RE NOT EVEN THAT GOOD AT THAT ANYMORE, ARE THEY?
SHOULD THE SENTINELS PURSUE?
NO.
OLD CHO MAY STILL HAVE ENOUGH BRAINS TO BE PLANNING FOR THAT.
WE NEED THE SENTINELS HERE, DEFENDING THE FORTRESS, FOR JUST ANOTHER FEW DAYS.
AFTER THAT...
"...NOTHING ANY HAARG DOES WILL MATTER."
YES! ONCE WE GET TO THE FOREST, WE'RE HOME FREE!
WAIT--MY BROTHER! HE'S STILL IN THE FORTRESS! IS HE--?
I DON'T LIKE LEAVING HIM LIKE THIS EITHER...
...BUT HE'S ALL RIGHT FOR NOW.
THE PRIESTESS HATES THE HAARG. SHE TRIED TO KILL US--
BUT SHE'S KEEPING THOSE KIDS ALIVE.
WHY...WOULD THE PRIESTESS ONLY WANT CHILDREN?

I DON'T KNOW.
THEY'RE LESS POWERFUL...
...EASIER TO CAGE...
...EASIER TO...
WHAT?
NOTHING.
WHAT?
EASIER TO EXPERIMENT ON.
SHE'S GOT A BIGGER PLAN.
SKITTTZ
WHERE-- WHERE'D HE GO?!
THE SIGNAL ONLY EXTENDS A MILE.
HE'S FINE.
WE HAVE TO GO BACK!
WE BARELY MADE IT OUT ALIVE.
I DON'T CARE! WE HAVE TO GET HIM OUT OF THERE!
WE CAN'T DO IT ALONE.
WE'LL GET BANNER.
THE STRONGEST ONE THERE IS...

"...AND THEN WE'LL TAKE CARE OF EVERYTHING."
SKY PEOPLE.
FLOATING BY LIKE NOTHING DOWN HERE MATTERS.
PSH.
I'M SURE THEY'VE GOT THEIR OWN RESPONSIBILITIES. AND IF ANYONE'S ABLE TO KEEP THEIR PEOPLE SAFE...
...MORE POWER TO 'EM.
WHAT'S THIS?
THE STEPPES.
THE LAST PLACE ANYONE EVER SAW THE GREEN SCAR.
NOW KEEP YOUR EYES O--
HAARG!
IN THE ROCKS!
FIRE!
BRRZZZAAM
BRRZZAAAAAM
AH, IT'S JUST ONE OF THOSE KITS.
MROW?
WELL, IT'S STILL A HAARG.
KILL IT.
BRRZZZZZAAAM
HA HA HA!

WHA...?
MRRRAAAAAAAARRR!
NO!
GAAAAAAAAAGH!
IT'S A GAMMALINE.
MADE 'EM BY ACCIDENT A FEW CENTURIES AGO.
HARMLESS IF YOU LEAVE 'EM ALONE.
PRRRRRRRR
I GUESS... I COULD HAVE WARNED THEM.
BUT THEN THEY'D HAVE TRIED TO KILL US.
BUT IT STILL...
...FEELS BAD, RIGHT?
NO.
OKAY.

WHAT... WHAT HAPPENED HERE?
THE LAST BATTLE THE GREEN SCAR EVER FOUGHT.
A HUNDRED YEARS AGO, WE STOOD RIGHT HERE AND DEFENDED THE LAST SHADOW ELDERS AGAINST THE HORDE OF THE FIFTH IMPERIUM.
AND BANNER...
...BANNER DID WHAT BANNER DOES.
AS FAR AS I KNOW, HE HASN'T LET THE MONSTER OUT SINCE.
LOOK!

BANNER?
HE'S NOT HERE.
BUT THIS IS THE PLACE.
HOW DO YOU KNOW?
THAT'S *CAIERA.*
THE GREEN SCAR'S QUEEN.
AND *KORG.*
THE GREEN SCAR'S GREATEST ALLY.
WHO'S *THIS?*
THAT'S *JEN.*
BANNER'S COUSIN.
ON EARTH, WE CALLED HER *SHE-HULK.*

SHE LOOKS... STRONG.
YEAH.
BUT SHE WAS REALLY A DIFFERENT KIND OF STRONG.
SHE CAME TO HELP US FIGHT.
BUT IN THE END, SHE WENT ANOTHER WAY.
HELPED NEGOTIATE THE LONG PEACE BETWEEN THE THIRD AND FOURTH IMPERIA, FOR WHAT THAT'S WORTH.
SOMEHOW, SHE STILL BELIEVES IN LAW.
"BELIEVES"?
SHE'S... SHE'S STILL ALIVE?
SHE'S AN ORIGINAL HULK. IT'D BE HARD FOR HER NOT TO BE.
WAIT A MINUTE, WHAT HAPPENED? WHERE IS SHE?
LOOK, SHE'S NOT--
MROW!
BANNER...

HERE HE COMES.
JUST... DON'T MAKE HIM ANGRY.
WHAT MAKES HIM ANGRY?
UH...
...EVERYTHING?
HEY...
...SORRY FOR JUST BARGING IN LIKE THIS AFTER...
NINETY SEVEN YEARS?
AMADEUS.
BANNER.
AFTER ALL THIS TIME, YOU STILL WON'T CALL ME BRUCE?
EH. JUST... FEELS WEIRD.
AND WHO'S THIS?
SHE'S...
...MY GRAND-DAUGHTER.
DO YOU HAVE A NAME?
WE NEED YOUR HELP.
OH. WELL, I'D BE HAPPY TO--
I'M NOT TALKING TO YOU.
I'M TALKING TO THE HULK.

UH...
...WHAT SHE MEANS IS--
HNN...
KKRRRRRITTTK
RRRRRRRRMMMMMMBBBBLLLLL
BANNER! WAIT!

RRRRRMMMMMMMMMBBBMMM
I'M...
Y-YES?
...I'M SORRY...
...BUT THE HULK...
...IS UNAVAILABLE.

WAIT!
YOU HAVEN'T EVEN HEARD--
A THOUSAND YEARS AGO...
...I STOOD HERE WITH CAIERA.
WE STARED OUT OVER THE STEPPES...
...AND I SAID...
MAYBE WE SHOULD JUST GO.
"JUST... DISAPPEAR.
"NEVER FIGHT AGAIN.
"AND SHE TOLD ME..."
YOU DON'T HAVE TO FEAR YOURSELF.
SO WE WENT BACK TO SAVE THE WORLD.
YOU KNOW HOW THAT ENDED?

"SHE DIED.
"ALONG WITH THOUSANDS OF OTHERS.
"GONE IN AN INSTANT WHEN CROWN CITY FELL."
THAT WAS A LONG TIME AGO.
RIGHT NOW, THERE'S AN EVIL PRIESTESS.
SHE'S KILLING EVERY HAARG SHE FINDS.
EXCEPT THE LITTLE ONES.
SHE'S KIDNAPPED MY BROTHER.
AND YOU THINK I CAN HELP?
YOU'RE THE STRONGEST ONE THERE IS.
THAT'S THE PROBLEM.
WHAT WERE YOU THINKING, AMADEUS?
YOU KNOW WHAT I AM.
YES!
YOU'RE WHAT WE NEED!
OF COURSE.
IT'S THE SAME THING, GENERATION AFTER GENERATION.

PEOPLE DON'T REALLY WANT TO MAKE THINGS BETTER.
THEY JUST WANT TO MAKE THINGS WORSE FOR THE PEOPLE THEY HATE.
THAT'S ALL THEY WANT THE HULK FOR.
PUNISHING.
THAT'S... THAT'S NOT WHAT I'M TALKING ABOUT!
I JUST WANT TO SAVE MY BROTHER!
OF COURSE.
HOW DARE YOU?

I CARRY YOUR CURSE.
BUT ALL IT GIVES ME IS THE STRENGTH TO ENDURE.
YOU...YOU HAVE ALL THE STRENGTH IN THE WORLD!
YOU COULD CHANGE THINGS! YOU COULD--
PRRRRRRRRRRRRRWWWWWBBBBRRLLL
YOU BETTER GO.
FINE.
WE'LL FIND HER.
THE SHE-HULK.
NO--
SHE'S A THOUSAND YEARS OLD. SHE CAN MAKE UP HER OWN MIND.
NO!
KKRRRAAK KOOOOOM

IF YOU KEEP PUSHING...
...WE'LL ALL DIE.
WHAT ARE YOU SCARED OF?
YOU'RE ALREADY DEAD.

THAT MIGHT NOT HAVE BEEN EXACTLY THE BEST WAY TO--
WHERE IS SHE?

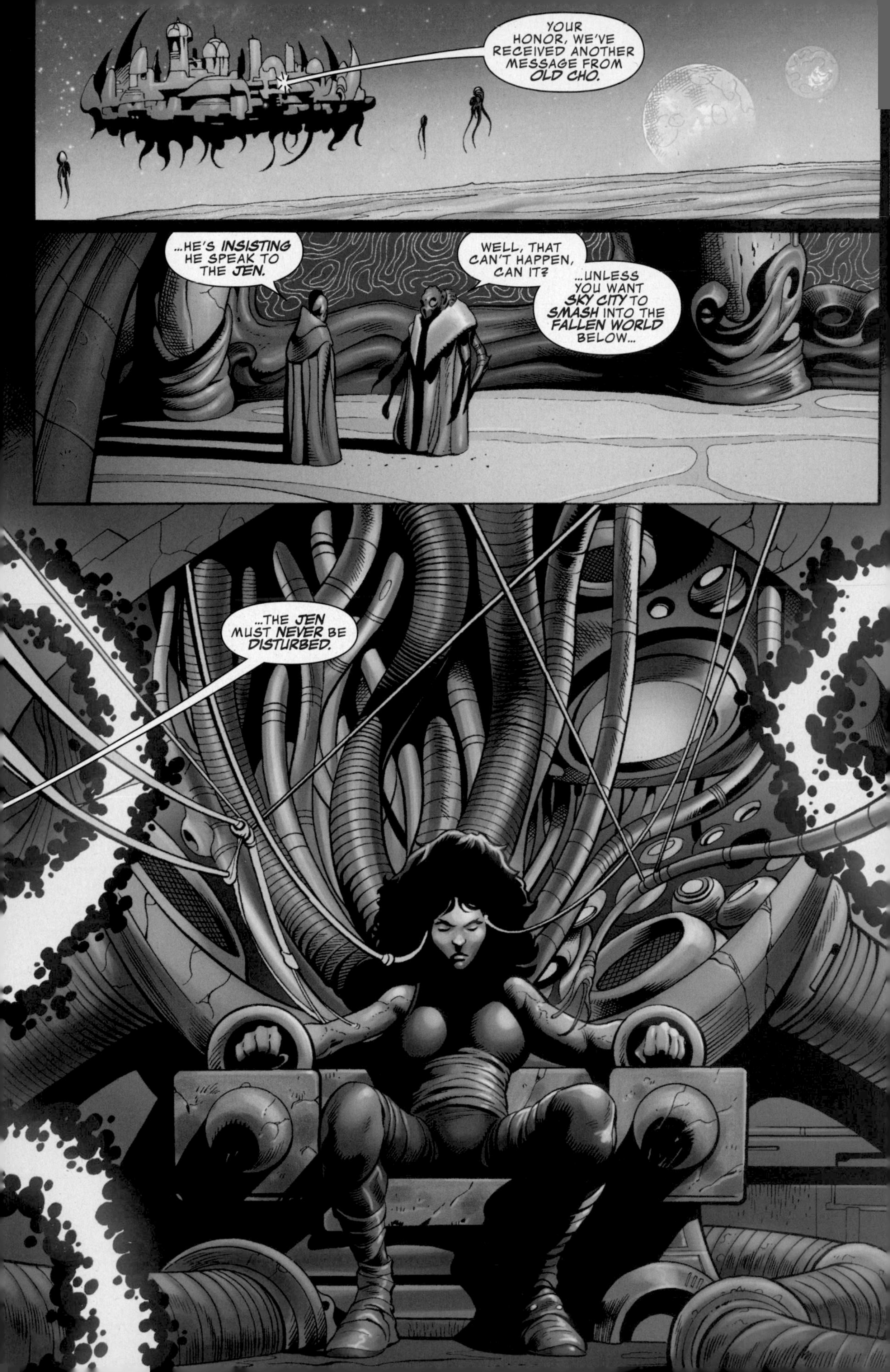
YOUR HONOR, WE'VE RECEIVED ANOTHER MESSAGE FROM OLD CHO.
...HE'S INSISTING HE SPEAK TO THE JEN.
WELL, THAT CAN'T HAPPEN, CAN IT?
...UNLESS YOU WANT SKY CITY TO SMASH INTO THE FALLEN WORLD BELOW...
...THE JEN MUST NEVER BE DISTURBED.

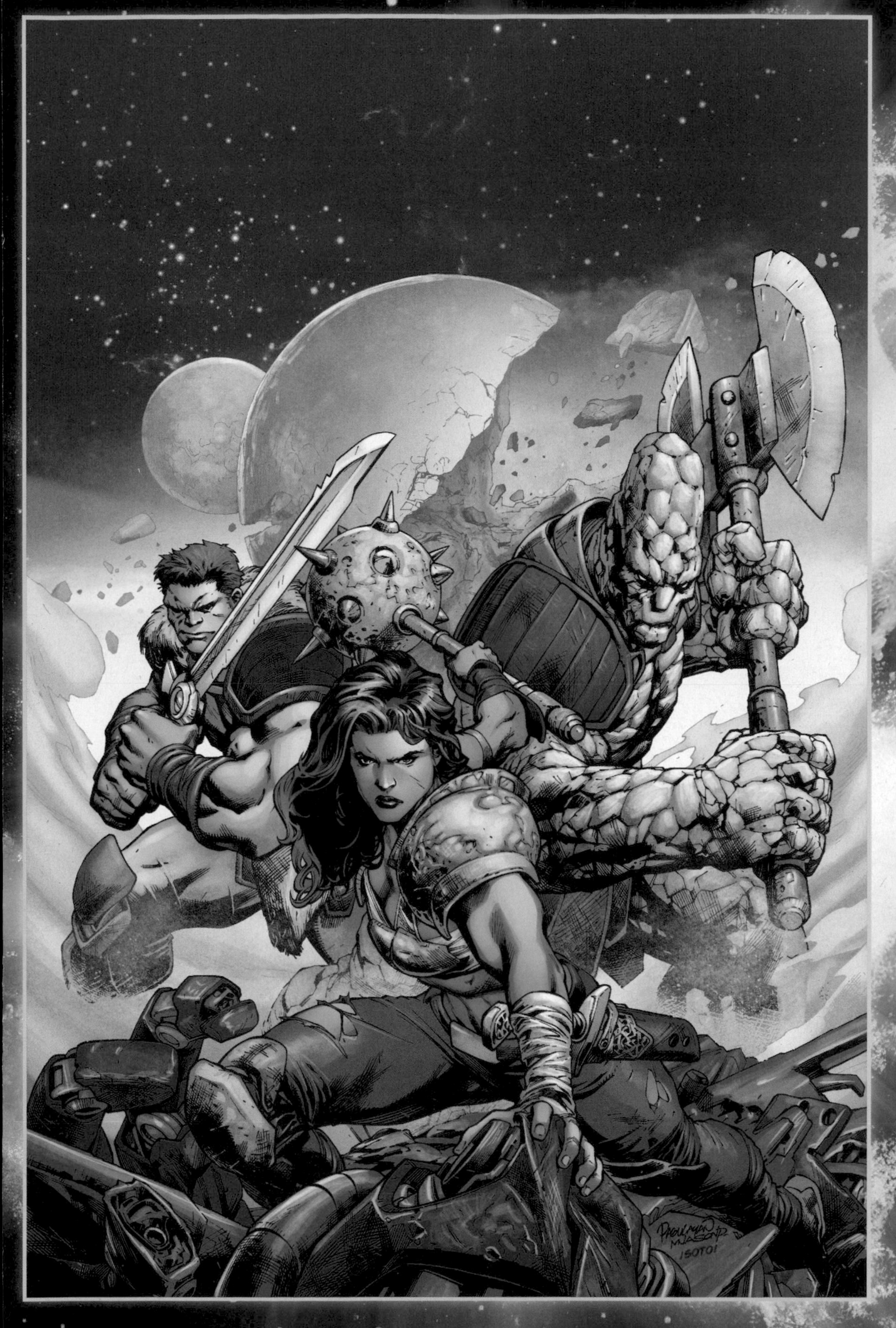

THREE

"THEY CALLED HER THE JEN.
"SAKAAR-CHILD.
"SHE-HULK.
"HAARGA.
"SHE HELPED MAKE THE LAST GREAT PEACE...
"...BUT SHE ALWAYS KNEW HOW TO SMASH."

AND WE'RE GONNA FIND HER, AND SHE'S GONNA SAVE YOU, BALO.
I KNOW YOU CAN'T HEAR ME.
BUT HANG ON, OKAY?
WE'RE COMING.
WAIT--
--THAT THING'S BACK ON?
DON'T WORRY, GRANDPA CHO. YOU TOLD ME YOURSELF-- THEY CAN'T HEAR US.
NO ONE KNOWS WHAT WE'RE PLANNING--

IT'S NOT THAT, KID! THE SIGNAL FROM THE CONNECTION COULD GET TRACKED!
DIDN'T ANYONE EVER TEACH YOU ABOUT THIS?
click
WHO WOULD HAVE?
YOU'RE THE ONLY ONE WHO KNOWS ABOUT THIS STUFF.
AND YOU WEREN'T THERE.
KTOOOOSH
YOU...
...YOU WERE BETTER OFF WITHOUT ME.
YOU'RE PROBABLY BETTER OFF WITHOUT ME NOW.
WHAT ARE YOU TALKING ABOUT?
FOR A LONG TIME, I TRIED...
...TO FIX EVERYTHING, ALL THE TIME.
YOU KNOW WHY I'M GREEN?

BECAUSE I TRIED TO FIX THE HULK.
I TOOK HIS GAMMA POWERS, THINKING I'D KNOW HOW TO USE THEM.
DID I LEARN ANYTHING FROM THAT EXPERIENCE?
I WAS A THOUSAND YEARS YOUNGER THAN I AM NOW.
I DID NOT.
SO HERE ON SAKAAR, I SPREAD SOME OF THAT GREEN AROUND.
I FIGURED IF PEOPLE HAD A LITTLE MORE... ENDURANCE...
...FEWER PEOPLE WOULD DIE.
BUT NOW IT'S JUST TURNED PEOPLE LIKE YOUR BROTHER INTO TARGETS FOR THAT HIGH PRIESTESS.
WAIT, YOU... YOU MADE THE HAARG?
I GUESS.
SOME THROUGH SCIENCE.
SOME...
...THROUGH LOVE.
EW!
I KNOW, I KNOW.
BUT YOU REALLY ARE MY GRANDDAUGHTER.
YOU'VE GOT THAT CHO-FAMILY STUBBORNNESS DOWN PAT.
boop
WHAT?

YOU NEVER ASKED ME MY NAME.

IF... ...IF I ASK YOU...

...I'LL NEVER FORGET IT.

I CARRY TOO MANY NAMES AROUND, KID.
GLORY.
MADDY.
CINDY.
JIMMY.
HERC.
TURNS OUT, EVEN GODS CAN DIE.

YOU'D THINK AFTER A HUNDRED YEARS...
...A THOUSAND YEARS...
...IT'D HURT LESS.

SKRRRAAKOOOOM
OW!
DESTROY!
ALL!
HAARG!
RUN!
WHA--?
RUN!
KTHOOOOOM
AAAAH!
SKRANNCH
DESTROY!
GRANDPA!
NO!
STAY WHERE YOU ARE!
ALL!
I'M NOT LEAVING YOU.
YOU SHOULD THOUGH. YOU SHOULD.
MY GOD, DON'T MAKE MY SAME MISTAKES, KID. YOU DON'T WANNA--
HAARG!
OH NO.
AH, STILL SO SAD AND SCARED, SOFTSKIN?
DON'T WORRY--

SKRAAAAKOOOOOM
--NO ONE'S DYING TODAY.

KORG!
AMADEUS.
I GOT YOUR MESSAGE. BEEN A WHILE.
WHO'S THIS?
WHAT...
...WHAT'S YOUR NAME?
TALA.
TALA.
SNIFF
THIS IS A MISTAKE, YOU KNOW.
I... DON'T GET IT.
DON'T WORRY. IT'S FINE.
BUT YOU JUST SAID IT'S A MISTAKE.
HA.

SO...YOU'RE THE STONE MAN--THE WARBOUND WHO FOUGHT AT THE GREEN SCAR'S SIDE?
WELL, I SEE THEY'RE STILL TEACHING THE KIDS THE IMPORTANT THINGS.
AND YOU'VE BEEN LIVING ON SKY CITY ALL THIS TIME?
NOT EXACTLY.
I LOOK FOR PEOPLE WHO NEED HELP AND BRING THEM TO SKY CITY.
BUT THERE SEEM TO BE A LOT OF PEOPLE WHO NEED HELP THESE DAYS.
SO I'M GLAD YOU'RE HERE.
KORG, I TOLD YOU!
WE CAN'T HANDLE ANY MORE STRAYS!
THAT'S NOT THE KIND OF TALK I REMEMBER HEARING FROM YOUR FATHER'S FATHER...
...BACK WHEN I HELPED BUILD THIS CITY.
OLD CHO...
DON'T ACT SURPRISED, GOVERNOR. I'VE BEEN PINGING YOU FOR HOURS.
WHERE'S JEN?
SHE--SHE'S INDISPOSED.
WHATEVER. I WAS JUST BEING POLITE.
I ALREADY TRACKED HER GAMMA SIGNATURE. THIRD SUBLEVEL, RIGHT?
NO!
SHE--SHE CHOSE THIS!
TO KEEP US ALL ALIVE!

WHAT-- WHAT THE HELL IS THIS?
AS THE CITY GREW, WE NEEDED MORE ENERGY.
YOU'D DISAPPEARED. WE COULDN'T FIND YOU TO ASK FOR HELP.
SO JEN...
...BECAME THE JEN.
HOW-- HOW LONG--?
EIGHTY-THREE YEARS.
JEN... MY GOD...
AMADEUS...
...I THOUGHT YOU... RETIRED.
I'M HERE WITH TALA.
WE NEED YOUR HELP.
WELL, WELL.
YOU...
...LEARNED A NEW NAME.
WHAT'S... WHAT'S HAPPENING?
A LITTLE TOO MUCH...

GRRRAAAAAAAAAA!
NO! PLEASE!
SKRRAAANCH
YOU HAVE TO RETURN TO THE MACHINE--
--OR THE CITY WILL FALL!
SHAKOOOOOSSSH

YOU CAN'T-- YOU CAN'T ABANDON US!
I SWORE TO HELP PEOPLE.
BUT YOU KEPT SECRETS. FOR GENERATIONS. WHILE PEOPLE ON THE GROUND SUFFERED.

WE SWORE TO KEEP THIS CITY SAFE!
WHAT ABOUT THEM?

YOU'RE STILL AN ISLAND. SAFER THAN MOST.
YOU'LL HAVE TO PROTECT YOURSELVES UNTIL I GET BACK.
MAYBE IT WOULDN'T SEEM SO HARD IF YOU'D PROTECTED OTHERS ALL THESE YEARS.

TALA'S BROTHER IS BEING HELD WITH AT LEAST A DOZEN OTHER HAARG CHILDREN IN A PRISON IN THE BASE OF GRAND PRIESTESS VENKIERA'S FORTRESS.
WE INFILTRATED THE FACILITY WITH A KIRB, SO I'VE GOT PARTIAL SCHEMATICS--
NEVER MIND ALL THAT, AMADEUS.
JUST GET ME CLOSE...

"...AND DROP ME OFF."
FTOOM
SKRAAAAAAAK
SKRANNNCH
HEY, KIDS.
LET'S GET OUT OF HERE.
BRRRZZZAAAM
GAH!

BRRRRZZZAAAAAM
NNNNH!
HAAAA!
SKLLAAAAANG
THAT'S IT!
SKRRAAAANCH
THIS WAY! COME ON!
EVERYBODY!
BALO!
TOO SQUEEZY!
HA HA!
COME ON, GRANDPA!
JUST A MINUTE...

THERE'S NO EQUIPMENT HERE.
THEY WEREN'T STUDYING THESE KIDS.
SO WHY--?
HA HA HA!
VENKIERA!
YOU REALLY AREN'T THAT SMART ANY LONGER, ARE YOU, OLD CHO?
THE CHILDREN WERE BAIT.
FTOOOOOOM
WHA--?
GAH!
SHAAANK
VNNNNNNNNNNNN
WE HOOKED YOU FIRST. BUT YOU WERE TOO WEAK.
SO I LET YOU GO, HOPING YOU'D BRING ME THE GREEN SCAR...
...BUT THE SAKAAR-CHILD WILL DO JUST FINE.
AAAAAAAGH!
SKRAAAARAKKTTT

FWOOOOOOOSSSSH
GAAAH!
NO! GRANDPA!
GET UP!
C-CAN'T.
THEY'RE... THEY'RE LEECHING ENERGY FROM JEN.
SH-SHOULD HAVE SEEN IT C-COMING. ANOTHER MISTAKE.
S-SORRY, TALA.
NO. I'M SORRY. IF--IF I HADN'T...
STOP.
DON'T BE LIKE ME.
YOU SAVED YOUR BROTHER.
HOLD ONTO THAT.
HOLD ONTO HIM.
AND GET THE HELL OUT OF HERE.
HA HA HA!

THERE'S NOWHERE TO GO.
WHY...
...WHY DO YOU HATE US SO MUCH?
I WAS AT THE STEPPES...
...WHEN THE LAST SHADOW ELDERS STOOD AGAINST THE FIFTH IMPERIUM.
YOU... YOU WERE A SHADOW PRIEST?
I WAS.
THEN WE...WE SAVED YOU!
THE HAARG!
WE SAVED YOU!
WHY HUNT US NOW?
BECAUSE I SAW WHAT YOU CAN DO.

"EVERYTHING I WAS EVER TAUGHT SAID THAT THERE WAS REASON TO THE WORLD.
"THAT WHAT WE DO MATTERS.
"THAT EACH ONE OF US HAS A ROLE TO PLAY, A PURPOSE.
"BUT AGAINST THE POWER AND FURY OF THE HAARG...
"...NOTHING MATTERS.
"TEN THOUSAND IMPERIAL SOLDIERS DIED THAT DAY.
"THEY WERE MY ENEMIES.
"BUT THEY WERE FLESH AND BLOOD LIKE ME.
"NOT MONSTERS LIKE YOU."

WE...WE DIDN'T KILL THOSE PEOPLE.
THE FIFTH IMPERIUM BOMBED THE WHOLE BATTLEFIELD.
THEY KILLED THEIR OWN ARMY TRYING TO KILL US!
YOU THINK THAT MAKES A DIFFERENCE?
IF YOU HADN'T BEEN THERE, THOSE PEOPLE WOULD HAVE LIVED.
YOU KNOW ALL THIS, OLD CHO.
THAT'S WHY YOU DISAPPEARED FOR ALL THESE YEARS.
WITH ALL YOUR POWER...
...HOW MUCH DAMAGE HAVE YOU DONE?
MY GRANDPA SAVED THOUSANDS OF PEOPLE! MILLIONS!
AND HOW MANY DID HE HARM?
HOW MANY MISTAKES DID HE MAKE?
HOW MANY MISTAKES HAVE YOU MADE, LITTLE HAARG?
EVERYBODY MAKES MISTAKES. NO MATTER HOW CAREFUL WE ARE.
DOES THAT MEAN WE SHOULD NEVER DO ANYTHING?
WE SHOULD NEVER TRY TO HELP?
THAT WE SHOULD JUST...DIE?
EXACTLY.

SKRRRAAAAKKOOOOOM
KRRRRROOOOOSHHH
YOU'VE RUINED THIS FALLEN WORLD.
THE ONLY WAY TO CLEANSE IT OF YOU...
...IS TO DESTROY IT.
RRRRRUMMMMBBBLLLE
YOU...
...YOU DON'T KNOW WHAT YOU'RE DOING.
YOU'LL WAKE UP BANNER.
YOU'LL WAKE UP THE WORLD-BREAKER!
BELIEVE ME, OLD CHO...

"...I'M COUNTING ON IT."
RRRRRMMMMMBBBBBLLLE

FOUR

RRRRRMMMMMBBBBBLLLE
WHEN THE WORLD BREAKS...
...SOMEONE...
...SHOULD DO SOMETHING.
IT SHOULD BE YOU.
THE OLDSTRONG.
BOUND TO THE STONE AND SOUL OF THE WORLD.
BUT THEY'VE FORGOTTEN YOU.
BUT I REMEMBER.
I'LL REMEMBER YOU FOREVER...
...CAIERA...

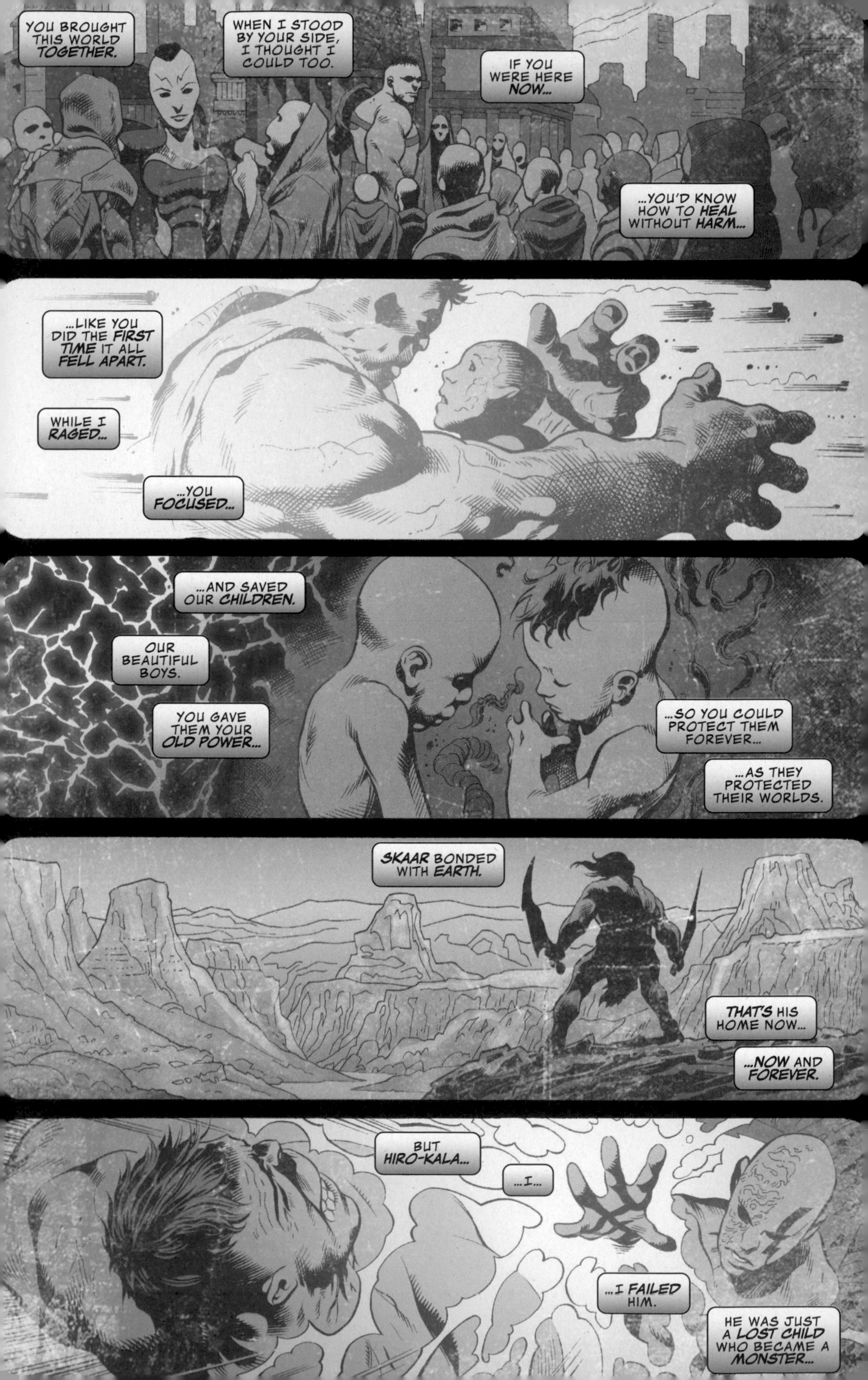
YOU BROUGHT THIS WORLD TOGETHER.
WHEN I STOOD BY YOUR SIDE, I THOUGHT I COULD TOO.
IF YOU WERE HERE NOW...
...YOU'D KNOW HOW TO HEAL WITHOUT HARM...
...LIKE YOU DID THE FIRST TIME IT ALL FELL APART.
WHILE I RAGED...
...YOU FOCUSED...
...AND SAVED OUR CHILDREN.
OUR BEAUTIFUL BOYS.
YOU GAVE THEM YOUR OLD POWER...
...SO YOU COULD PROTECT THEM FOREVER...
...AS THEY PROTECTED THEIR WORLDS.
SKAAR BONDED WITH EARTH.
THAT'S HIS HOME NOW...
...NOW AND FOREVER.
BUT HIRO-KALA...
...I...
...I FAILED HIM.
HE WAS JUST A LOST CHILD WHO BECAME A MONSTER...

I KNOW ALL ABOUT THAT.
I SHOULD HAVE BEEN ABLE TO REACH HIM.
AAAGH...
YOU ALWAYS KNEW HOW TO DO THE RIGHT THING, THE RIGHT WAY.
KRAAAACK
BUT I...
...I MÜCK IT UP...
...EVERY TIME.
ALL THE POWER IN THE WORLD...
...BUT WHENEVER I USE IT...
RRRRRRMMMMMMMMBBBBLLL
...I JUST BREAK THINGS.

THE FORTRESS OF GRAND PRIESTESS VENKIERA.
SKRRRRRRRAAAAAAKK
IT'S WORKING, YOUR HOLINESS!
BUT THE SHE-HAARG'S NEARLY DEAD!
GRRAAAAA!
GOOD.
REDIRECT HER REMAINING POWER TO THE ENGINES...
RRRUMMMMMMMMBBBLLL
...AND LET US FINALLY END THIS CURSED HAARGWORLD.
TALA! BALO! RUN!
UFF!
BALO!

I'M SORRY, TALA.
WHAT ARE YOU TALKING ABOUT?
I GOT CAUGHT, AND NOW WE'RE IN TROUBLE.
YOU GOT CAUGHT BECAUSE YOU WERE TRYING TO SAVE ME.
BUT--
WE CAN'T CONTROL EVERYTHING.
WE CAN'T PREDICT EVERYTHING THAT'S GONNA HAPPEN.
WE'RE JUST DOING OUR BEST.
AND I LOVE YOUR BEST.
AMADEUS!
THEY'VE GOT JEN!
THEY USED HER TO BREAK THE GROUND--AND NOW SHE'S POWERING THEIR SHIP!
I...I HAVE TO CALL BANNER.
YEAH, WE NEED HIM...
YES! TELL HIM WE NEED HIM!

"...TO STAY EXACTLY WHERE HE IS."
BANNER?
AMADEUS.
THE TECTONIC PLATES ARE SHIFTING.
IT'S THE PRIESTESS, ISN'T IT?
YOU JUST HANG TIGHT.
WE'VE GOT THIS.
NO. IT'S ALREADY GONE TOO FAR.
WHERE ARE YOU?
NO, BANNER!
WHO'S BANNER?
THE GREEN SCAR.
THE GREEN SCAR?
HE'S STRONG.
I KNOW.
GRANDPA, IF BANNER WANTS TO HELP US NOW--
NO, TALA. VENKIERA IS JUST TRYING TO DRAW HIM OUT SO SHE CAN TAP HIS POWER.
AND THEN WHO KNOWS WHAT SHE'LL DO.
JUST STAY WHERE YOU ARE, BANNER.
BUT...
YOU WERE JUST TALKING ABOUT ALL THE TIMES WE SCREWED UP!
AND YOU...
...YOU WERE JUST HERE ASKING FOR HELP ANYWAY.
FORGET ALL THAT.
UFF. IT'S NOT YOUR FAULT...

...BUT THIS IS TOO MUCH.
THIS PRIESTESS REALLY WANTS TO DESTROY THE WORLD.
AND IF SHE PULLS YOU INTO THIS FIGHT...
...I THINK SHE ACTUALLY COULD.
I'M... I'M SORRY, BANNER, BUT YOU'RE JUST--
CHO!
IT'S THE JEN!
CAN I BORROW THAT AX?

GRRAAAAAA!
SKAAAANNG
FTOOOOM
UKK!
FTOOOOM
NNGH!
FTOOOOM
THEY'RE RUNNING AWAY!
BUT THE WORLD...
"...THE WORLD'S STILL BREAKING."
AAGH!
OH NO...

AAAAAH!
WH-WHAT'S HAPPENING?!
IT'S THE END! THE CURSE OF THE HAARG! JUST LIKE THE HIGH PRIESTESS FORETOLD!
HEADMAN! WHAT ARE YOU DOING? LET US ON!
SHE WARNED YOU, AND YOU DENIED HER--SO YOU CAN STAY!
WHAT?!
DON'T WORRY, FRIENDS...
...YOU DON'T HAVE TO BELIEVE THOSE LIES TO BOARD THIS BOAT!
COME ON, EVERYONE!
BUT YOU'RE... YOU'RE HAARG!
UGH. NOT THIS AGAIN.
FWOOOOSSSH
HA HA HA HA! THAT'S RIGHT!

THE HAARG CAUSED ALL OF THIS!
AND NOW YOU'LL DIE WITH THEM!
THEY'RE LYING! IT WAS THE PRIESTESS WHO SET OFF THE QUAKES!
NOW GET ON BEFORE IT'S TOO--
HOW COULD THE PRIESTESS HAVE DONE THIS?
THE HAARG ARE THE ONLY PEOPLE WITH THE POWER TO BREAK THE WORLD!
SKRRRRAAAAKK
AAAAAH!
OR THE POWER TO SAVE YOUR ASS.
FFFSSSSSSSSST
AAAAAAH!
UFF.
THE LAVA'S EVERYWHERE.
WE NEED OUR OWN STARSHIP.
WAIT A MINUTE...

"...WE'VE GOT OUR OWN FLOATING CITY!"
CHO! WHAT IS GOING ON HERE?
THE PRIESTESS IS DESTROYING THE WORLD...
...SO WE TOLD ALL THE NEIGHBORING SETTLEMENTS TO COME HERE.
WE'RE SAVING EVERYONE.
HOW?
THE ISLAND CAN'T FLY WITHOUT A JEN...
...AND YOU'VE APPARENTLY USED THIS ONE ALL UP.
WELL...
...SHE'S NOT THE ONLY HAARG IN TOWN.
GRANDPA!

NO!
YOU'RE TOO WEAK-- YOU GOT DRAINED BY VENKIERA'S MACHINES TOO!
LET ME DO IT!
THAT'S THE SPIRIT, KID.
BUT I'VE JUST TWEAKED THE MACHINERY SO IT VERY SPECIFICALLY WON'T WORK WITH YOU.
WHAT?
YOU'RE THE WHOLE REASON I'M BACK AT THIS, TALA.
YOU'RE NOT DYING TODAY.
SO YOU ARE?!
ALL OF THIS...IS MY FAULT.
NO.
IT'S LIKE EVERYONE'S BEEN SAYING.
IT'S NOT JUST BANNER. WE'RE...WE'RE ALL WORLDBREAKERS, AREN'T WE?
NO. NO.
WE'RE JUST... PEOPLE.
WE HAVE TO BE A LITTLE MORE CAREFUL...
...BUT WE ALL HAVE OUR TURN... TO DO WHAT WE HAVE TO.
I'M HOPING YOURS WON'T COME FOR A LONG, LONG TIME.
BUT NOW...
HHHHHNNNNNNNNNNNN
...IT'S MINE.
GRANDPA!

WHAT'S GOING ON? THE LAVA'S NEARLY GOT US!
DON'T WORRY. OLD CHO WON'T LET YOU--
FFFFSSSSSSSSSS
RRRRRUMMMMMMBBBBBLL
OH NO...
YAAAAAAA!
NNNGGGH...
GRANDPA!
WHAT'S HAPPENING?
HE'S NOT STRONG ENOUGH!
HE'LL ONLY KEEP US ALOFT A FEW HOURS BEFORE HE DIES...
AND THEN I'LL GO BACK IN.
SO YOU CAN DIE TOO?
NO.
TALA--
HE SAID WE ALL HAVE OUR TURN.
NOW...
...IT'S BANNER'S.

HELLO...
SHHHAAAKOOOOOM
YOU'RE BACK.
ARE YOU?
NO!

TALA...
GRANDPA--
PLEASE...
NO.
IT'S NOT ENOUGH JUST TO KEEP THE CITY FLYING.
VENKIERA'S TRYING TO DESTROY EVERYTHING.
BANNER'LL FIGURE THAT OUT...
...AND THEN HE'LL FIGHT.
AND THEN GOD ONLY KNOWS...
YOU...
...YOU USED TO BELIEVE IN ME, AMADEUS.
HELL, YOU USED TO BELIEVE IN YOURSELF.
A THOUSAND YEARS AGO...
...UNDER MANHATTAN...
"...YOU TOLD ME WE HAD ENOUGH BRAINS TO TALLY UP ALL THE VARIABLES...
"...TO FOCUS OUR POWER PERFECTLY TO AVOID HURTING INNOCENTS."
CAN'T...
...CAN'T WE DO THAT AGAIN?

THAT WAS A FANTASY, EVEN BACK THEN.
WE MANAGED IT FOR A WHILE.
BUT YOU CAN'T SEE OR CONTROL EVERY SINGLE FACTOR.
FFFSSSSS
THERE'S NO SUCH THING AS PERFECTION.
FFWUMP
NO GUARANTEE OF SAFETY OR SUCCESS.
FFFSSS
AND WITH ALL THE POWER THAT YOU CAN UNLEASH...
IT'S ALL RIGHT, GRANDPA.
YOU JUST HAVE TO...
...DO YOUR BEST.

AND I LOVE YOUR BEST.
THAT'S WHAT TALA SAYS.
SOUNDS GOOD TO ME.

THIS SHOULD BE YOU.
IT'S A JOB FOR A MAKER...
...NOT A BREAKER.
FRRAAKOOOOOOOM

BUT WE'RE ALL THAT WE'VE GOT.
AND THAT'S GOING TO HAVE TO BE ENOUGH.

HEADMAN, WE HAVE WORD FROM THE WASTELAND...
...THE GREEN SCAR HAS RETURNED!
WHAA--?
NO NEED TO WORRY.
WE'VE ESCAPED TO THE GRAND PRIESTESS' FORTRESS--
--THE IMPREGNABLE STONE STARSHIP OF THE OLD SHADOW!
THE HULK CAN'T DESTROY US NOW!
YOU'RE CONFUSED, HEADMAN.
YOUR...YOUR HOLINESS?
YOU'RE NOT HERE TO ESCAPE. YOU'RE HERE TO FIGHT.
BECAUSE THE HULK IS TRYING TO SAVE THIS CURSED WORLD.
SAVE?
I THOUGHT-- I THOUGHT HE WAS THE WORLDBREAKER.
OH, NO, HEADMAN...
...THAT'S US.

FIVE

GREEN SCAR...
...THE PRIESTESS IS BREAKING THE PLANET.
WE NEED TO FIND WHATEVER MACHINE SHE'S USING TO DO IT.
SAKAAR. A THOUSAND YEARS FROM NOW.
AMADEUS, NO ONE'S GOT A BIGGER BRAIN FOR THIS KIND OF THING.
IT'S TIME TO TRIANGULATE THE TECTONIC WAVES OR WHATEVER YOU DO.
I...I HAVEN'T BEEN ABLE TO PULL THOSE KINDS OF TRICKS FOR CENTURIES, JEN.
YOU MEAN YOU HAVEN'T TRIED.
I...TOLD YOU. WE CAN'T SEE ALL THE VARIABLES.
IF I DO THIS AND SOMETHING GOES WRONG...
ALL I KNOW...
...IS THAT EVERYTHING WILL GO WRONG IF YOU DON'T.
JUST DO YOUR BEST, GRANDPA.
OKAY, TALA.
OKAY.
HNN...

A HUNDRED STONE STEPS TO THE SOUTH.
THIS...THIS IS MADNESS! WE'RE NOT WARRIORS!
BUT WE CAN'T STAND AGAINST THE HAARG!
THE PRIESTESS COMMANDS IT, HEADMAN. THE WORLD MUST BE PURGED. AND WE MUST HOLD THE LINE UNTIL IT'S DONE.
CALM YOURSELVES, MY PEOPLE.
AND BE RECONCILED.
EVERY ONE OF US, NO MATTER HOW INNOCENT OR SANCTIFIED...
...HAS DONE...
...UNFORGIVABLE THINGS.
THIS CRUEL WORLD WASN'T BUILT FOR MORTALS...OR OUR WEAKNESSES.
BUT NOW WE WILL BE RELEASED.
AND THE WORLD REBORN...
...PURGED OF THE MONSTERS...
...AND THE MONSTERS THEY MADE OF US.
BUT WE'RE... WE'RE NOT MONSTERS!
THAT'S THE HAARG!
YES.
AND EVERY TIME WE IMPRISONED OR EXILED OR KILLED ONE OF THEM...
...WE DÖOMED OUR OWN SOULS.
NOW GO...

...JOIN THE SENTINELS.
HOLD OFF THE HAARG ONE LAST TIME.
AND LET A PERFECT WORLD BE BORN WITHOUT US.
HIGH PRIESTESS!
THEY'VE FOUND US!
FINALLY.
DESTROY ALL HAARG!
DESTROY ALL HAARG!
DESTROY--

GRRRRRRRRAAAAAAAA!
SKRAAAAKOOOOOOOOOM

SKRRRRRAAAKKTTT
DESTROY ALL HAARG!
DESTROY ALL--
FRRANOOOOOOOOM
FSSSSSSSTTTTTT
KRAAKOOOOM
BRRRAKOOOOOOOM
SKRRRRAAKOOOOW
GRRRRRRAAAAAAAA!
WAIT, HULK!

SMASH AS MANY SENTINELS AS YOU WANT...
...BUT THOSE...
...THOSE ARE JUST PEOPLE.
GO AHEAD, HAARG.
GIVE THEM WHAT THEY DESERVE.
JUST LAY DOWN YOUR WEAPONS AND WALK AWAY!
NO ONE HAS TO DIE TODAY! NO ONE DESERVES THAT! NO MATTER WHAT THAT PRIESTESS SAYS!
EVEN SHE CAN WALK AWAY!
P-PRIESTESS...?
FINE.
I'LL GET US STARTED.
AAAAAGH!
SKRRRAAAAKKT

GRRAAAAAAAA!
KTHOOOOOOOOM
THAT'S IT, GREEN SCAR!
JUST SMASH!
WE'LL FINISH THIS TOGETHER!
HEADMAN, THE LAVA! THE PRIESTESS SENT IT FOR US!
AAAAAAH!
NO!
CHO! THE MACHINE! NOW!
FOOOOOOOOM
ALL RIGHT, HULK...

...THAT'S WHERE SHE'S HIDDEN IT.
SO, HOW DO WE STOP IT?
I'VE BEEN TRYING TO FIGURE THAT OUT EVER SINCE I EXTRAPOLATED ITS EXISTENCE, JEN...
...AND I DON'T KNOW THAT I'VE COME UP WITH A BETTER IDEA...
...THAN SMASHING IT.
BUT--
WORKS FOR ME.
HULK!
SKRRAAAKOOOOOM
SKRRRAAAKOOOOOOOOOM
WAIT!

RRRRRRRRRRRRRRRRRUMMMMM
DO YOU FEEL THAT, SOFTSKINS?
THE GROUND...
IT'S SETTLING.
L-LOOK!
SSSSSSSSSSSSS
YES! THE LAVA'S RECEDING!
WE'RE...
"...WE'RE SAVED!"
YEEEEEAAAAAAA!

OH NO.
OH NO, NO, NO...
WHAT IS IT, AMADEUS?
CAN'T YOU FEEL IT?
NOW IT'S TOO... ...IT'S TOO STILL.
RRRKMMMBBBLLLL
I KNEW THERE WAS SOMETHING-- SOME VARIABLE I COULDN'T SEE...
AAH!
THE PRIESTESS' MACHINE WASN'T JUST SPLITTING THE SURFACE.
IT WAS TRYING TO STOP THE MOLTEN CORE OF THE PLANET FROM SPINNING.
AND WE JUST GAVE IT THE LAST BIT OF ENERGY IT NEEDED.
BUT WHAT... ...WHAT DOES THAT MEAN?
SHRRAAAAAAROOOOOM
IT MEANS IT'S OVER, HAARG!
HA HA HA HA HA!

WITHOUT THE DYNAMO OF THE MOLTEN CORE...
...THE PLANET'S PROTECTIVE MAGNETOSPHERE IS BREAKING APART.
SO...
COSMIC RAYS.
INCINERATING EVERYTHING.
FINALLY...
...OUR TIME IS DONE.
TALA... BALO...
GRANDPA...
I'M SO--
SKRRBRAAAAAAKKTT

NO!
TALA!
BRRRZZZZZZAAAAAAM
AAAAAAAGH!
GRRRRRRAAAAAAGH!
SHE--SHE'S ALIVE!
THIS IS WHAT SHE DOES.
SHE CAN ABSORB SO MUCH PUNISHMENT.
AND SHE NEVER GIVES UP.
BUT THIS...
...THIS IS TOO MUCH.

SKRRRRAAAAAAAAAAK

ENOUGH.
HULK... WHAT ARE YOU--?
ENOUGH.
TOO MANY PEOPLE...
...BURNING...
...WHEN IT SHOULD JUST BE ME.
SKRRAA
AKOOOOOM

THIS IS THE STORY OF THE GREEN SCAR.
THE EYE OF ANGER.
THE WORLD-BREAKER.
OR MAYBE...

...THIS IS THE STORY OF A MONSTER...
...OR JUST A MAN...
FOOL!
...DEEPLY FLAWED...
...BROKEN AND BREAKING...
LEAVE ME ALONE!
...THE CAUSE OF SO MUCH PAIN...
SKAAR...
...AND THE TARGET OF SO MUCH PAIN...
CAIERA!
...BUT AFTER ALL THESE YEARS...
...STILL DESPERATELY TRYING TO MAKE THINGS RIGHT...
...DESPITE HIMSELF AND EVERYTHING ELSE IN THE WORLD.

DO WE ALWAYS KNOW WHAT THE RIGHT THING IS?
RRRRRRRRRRMMMMMMMBBLLL
GAH!
DO WE KNOW IF IT WILL WORK?
SKKTTTTTTKT
NO.
FFFFSSSSSSSS
NNNGH...
MY GOD. THE CORE...
...HE...
HE SMASHED IT.
AND FIRED IT UP AGAIN!
OF COURSE HE DID.
BUT THIS IS THE STORY OF EVERYONE...

...OF YOU...
...OF ME.
LIVING IN A BROKEN WORLD.
CONTINUALLY SHATTERED AND REBORN.
MAKING NEW MISTAKES EVERY DAY.
BUT ALWAYS...

HA!
...ALWAYS...
...ALWAYS...
...LOOKING FOR ANOTHER REASON...

...TO TRY AGAIN.
END.

NEW MEXICO.

BANNER?
DNA MATCH LOCK: ACTIVATED.
CLACK

DAD?

WHERE...
SKTTTTT

...WHERE ARE YOU?

SKAAR...
...WHAT ARE YOU DOING?
WHO--?

IT'S JUST ME.
AUNTIE JEN.
I HEARD YOU'D TEAMED UP WITH GAMMA FLIGHT.* BUT THEN YOU DISAPPEARED.
I FIGURED I SHOULD COME FIND YOU.
LOOKING A LITTLE DIFFERENT, THESE DAYS. INCOGNITO, HUH?
*CHECK OUT THE MINISERIES GAMMA FLIGHT (2021) FOR MORE DETAILS! --DK
BUT HERE YOU ARE USING YOUR OLD POWER.
WHAT'S GOING ON?
I'M... LOOKING FOR MY FATHER.
YYYEAH. I TRIED THAT TOO. PRETTY SURE HE'S OFF-PLANET AT THE MOMENT.
HE...HE TOLD ME HE'D NEVER LEAVE ME.
THEN HE DIED.
THEN HE CAME BACK...
...BUT HE NEVER TRIED TO FIND ME AGAIN.
HE'S...
...HE'S BROKEN A LOT OF THINGS IN HIS LIFE.
MAYBE HE THOUGHT YOU'D BE BETTER--
I DON'T CARE WHAT HE THOUGHT.
HE...HE LOVES YOU, SKAAR.
I DON'T KNOW IF YOU REMEMBER...
...BUT IN HIS WILL, HE PROMISED TO REBUILD THE STONE STARSHIP OF YOUR MOTHER'S PEOPLE.
THE PLANS ARE HERE. IF YOU WANT, WE COULD--
SO YOU CAN GET RID OF ME, TOO?

WHAT?
I KNOW WHAT YOU'RE SAYING.
NO ONE WANTS ME. NO ONE NEEDS ME.
I'M TOO MUCH LIKE HIM.
I DON'T BELONG HERE.

SKAAR...
...YOU...YOU BELONG... WHEREVER YOU WANT TO BELONG.
THAT'S NOT TRUE.

SAKAAR DOESN'T WANT ME.
WHAT ARE YOU TALKING ABOUT?
YOU DON'T KNOW WHAT I DID THERE.
SKAAR--
SO I'M STUCK HERE.

BUT WHEN I REACH OUT THROUGH THE STONES OF THIS PLANET...
...ALL I SEE ARE PUNY HUMANS...
...WHO'D HATE ME AS MUCH AS SAKAAR DOES IF THEY KNEW WHAT I REALLY AM.

AND WHAT'S THAT?
THE SON OF HULK.
THE WORLDBREAKER.
YOU'RE... YOU'RE JUST A KID, SKAAR.
YOU'RE NOT BOUND BY ANY OF THAT OLD--
WAIT...

GRRRAAAAAAAA!
9-1-1. WHAT'S YOUR--?
WE'RE DOWN ON THE BLIGHT ROAD SIDE OF THE MAYHEW PROPERTY!
THERE'S-- THERE'S THIS THING--
--A MONSTER!
A MONSTER?
BOSS, LOOK!
KID! WHAT ARE YOU DOING?!
GET OUT OF THERE!
RRRRRAAAAAAA!
SHHHHH.

GRRRAAAAAAAA!

CREEEEAAK

IT'S ALL RIGHT.
YOU'RE FREE NOW.
KRRRRR...

DON'T WORRY. THEY CAN'T HURT YOU ANYMORE.
RRRRRR...
WE'LL GET YOU SOMEWHERE SAFE, AND--

VZZZZ
TTTZZAM
GRRAAKK!

THANKS FOR THE DISTRACTION, KID.
NOW GET OUT OF THE WAY SO WE CAN FINISH THE JOB.
WHO...
...WHO ARE YOU?
B.A.N.
BUREAU OF ALIEN NEUTRALIZATION.
WE PROTECT THE PLANET FROM INVASIVE SPECIES.
B.A.N.
INVASIVE SPECIES...
...YOU MEAN...
...LIKE ME?
WHAT THE--?
FIRE!

GRRRAAAAAAAAA!
AAAAAGH!
VZZAAAAM
VTITZZAAAM
VZZZZAAAM

VAAAZZZAAM
GAH!
RRRRRRR!
SKRAAANCH
GAH!
GRRRRRRAAAAA!
AAAH!
KAPOW
UKK!

NNNNNH...
OKAY. NO CHOPPING NECESSARY.
RIGHT?
RIGHT.

YOU'RE IN BIG TROUBLE, LADY!
MAYBE.
OR MAYBE YOU DON'T HAVE THE PROPER AUTHORIZATION TO EVEN BE IN THIS JURISDICTION.

RRRRRRR...
SO YOU CAN MAKE FRIENDS.
HE'S FROM SAKAAR. PROBABLY GOT LOST BACK DURING MY FATHER'S WAR.

WELL, THAT EXPLAINS THEIR INTEREST.
WHAT?
THIS WHOLE THING'S A MESS.
I KNOW ENOUGH FRIENDLY JUDGES TO STALL THESE JOKERS FOR A WHILE...

...BUT THEY'RE NOT GOING AWAY.
THEY'VE GOT AN OFFICIAL MANDATE AND A LIST OF TARGETS.
ALIENS OF ALL KINDS.

LOOK, I WAS TRYING TO TELL YOU...
...YOU'RE JUST A KID. NONE OF THIS IS YOUR FAULT.
BUT MAYBE WE REALLY SHOULD FIRE UP THAT STARSHIP.
FIND A PLACE WHERE YOU CAN GROW UP IN PEACE.

I SAID I DIDN'T BELONG HERE.
NO ONE WANTS ME.
NO ONE NEEDS ME...
KKRRR...

"...BUT MAYBE I WAS WRONG."
SKAAR, SON OF HULK!
WRITER: GREG PAK ARTIST: RAMÓN F. BACHS COLORIST: CHRIS SOTOMAYOR LETTERER: VC's JOE CARAMAGNA

#1 VARIANT BY **LEINIL FRANCIS YU** & **SUNNY GHO**

#1 VARIANT BY **ADAM KUBERT** & **BRAD ANDERSON**

#1 VARIANT BY **RYAN BROWN**

#1 SKAAR VARIANT BY **GIUSEPPE CAMUNCOLI** & **FRANK MARTIN**

#2 VARIANT BY **GARY FRANK** & **BRAD ANDERSON**

#2 VARIANT BY **GEOFF SHAW** & **DEAN WHITE**

#3 VARIANT BY **ED McGUINNESS** & **LAURA MARTIN**

#3 VARIANT BY **NICK BRADSHAW**
& **JIM CHARALAMPIDIS**

#4 VARIANT BY **KEN LASHLEY**
& **JUAN FERNANDEZ**